Praise for *Soap Is Political*

In these unusual and evocative poems, Ruth Goring exposes a Colombia far more complex, anguished, and painfully beautiful than anything you will read in the news. The tragic and horrifying become everyday, and the everyday is revealed in its tragedy and horror. We are taken to the heart of Colombia's war against the poor with a language that is lush and compelling. If you want to experience Colombia's conflicts with all of your senses as well as your intellect, Goring's poetry will take you there.

—**Avi Chomsky**

SOAP IS POLITICAL

POEMS
RUTH GORING

GLASS LYRE PRESS

Copyright © 2015 Ruth Goring
Paperback ISBN: 978-1-941783-05-4

All rights reserved: except for the purpose of quoting brief passages for review, no part of this book may be reproduced or transmitted in any form or by any means, electronic or mechanical, including photocopying, recording, or by any information storage and retrieval system, without permission in writing from the publisher.

Cover art: Ruth Goring
Cover & interior design/layout: Steven Asmussen
Copyediting: Elizabeth Nichols
Author photo: Michael Bracey

Glass Lyre Press, LLC.
P.O. Box 2693
Glenview, IL 60026

www.GlassLyrePress.com

Contents

Prelude
Painting with water	9
Why	11

Rain
Flood	17
Arrival	19
Seis	20
Eucalyptus	21
Maternal gestures	22
Arithmetic	23
Inheritance	24
Ride	25

Tongue
Tal vez	29
Bilingual	30
Bilingüe	31
For example	32
Coco	34
Numbers	35
A former sergeant explains	36
las listas de exterminación	
Presidential qualities	37
Ashore	39
Nights, days	41
Perancho	42

Color of Earth

    Syllogism   47

    Nueva Vida chirimía   48

    Braids   49

    Portrait   51

    Stung   52

    Ecosystem   53

    Incursion   54

    Sabbath   56

Planting Our Names

    Under   61

    New stones   62

    Shrine   64

    Geography of a saint   66

    Family stories   67

    Las horas del corazón   69

    Ayer   70

    Yesterday   71

    Testigo   72

    Witness   73

    Our voices, our hands   74

WHAT OUR MOTHER TAUGHT US

Soap is political	81
Excavation	83
Beholding	85
After you	86
La Niña	87
This war	88
Judith tells me stories	91
What our mother taught us	93
Canción de cuna	98
Lullaby	99
Extranjera	100

GLOSSARY 103

ACKNOWLEDGMENTS 109

PAINTING WITH WATER
for Oscar Muñoz, artist

Oscar's works are shown
in time-lapse film. He dips his brush
and paints a face on a flat stone:
cheekbones, hungry mouth,
eyes that do not blink.
The sun then does its part,
laps up the water—
cheek, chin cleft, blunt gaze
—with hot impartial tongue.

The stone shrugs imperceptibly,
knows nothing of the disappeared.
It is for us to speak their names.

Why

You carved roots into me, Colombia, you snared me with generous branches, the child receives everything, bananas and papaya, guava sweets, such plentiful limes, *arroz con pollo*, balconies, *cuadernos*, outhouses (or just the bushes), an iron holding hot coals, *chirimoyas*, empanadas, sweetened condensed milk, laundry on lines and fences or spread on rocks, *cuys* squeaking beneath the floorboards, candle flame to read by, the birth and death of puppies, road puddles, buses, taxis, cumbia, *vallenato*, Argentinian pop music on the radio, the stares, the city lights, the longing.

Years later when I came home to Spanish: the starved places in my mouth and gut, suddenly replete. Ecstasy.

You pained me too: distended bellies, tiny coffins, burgled houses, burgled faces. *Actores armados* (*insurgente, militar, paramilitar*), the lexicon of war: *requisar, descuartizar, ametralladora, desaparecido, glifosato, desplazada*. Narcotrafficking and its brutalities, its American sources, its American market. The plastic surgery craze; the vengeful disfigurements with acid. The mass graves.

You gave me new hero words: *movilizar, denunciar, comunidad de resistencia, comunidad de paz*.

The slow steps toward a peace agreement. The need for imagination, for courageous realism: what to do with *los mochas*, men known as the choppers? what can a country do with so much blood?

For you, these poems. I am asking with you.

* * *

A note on names and narrative: Sometimes where a poem is honoring a particular martyr or public figure, his or her full name is given. I've shortened the names of many living persons, however, or changed them altogether to protect their safety. Likewise the events narrated here are based on fact, but I have imagined many of the details.

Rain

Flood
Nueva Vida, Cacarica, Chocó
August 2004

We all went to church that night
a Tuesday, as a rainstorm walloped
the new zinc roof. Candle flames
shuddered among shadows cast
by a kerosene lamp. Hymns rose
from the dark rows of chairs,
prayers flinched and dodged
the pounding, swam
toward each amen.
We dripped, strained, sang
and Javier loomed in the back
with his great cloak.

Clatter cacophony
rain hullabaloo rain rain—
it is too large, Lord,
we will be smithereens.

The rain is hammers.
The rain is *chirimía*.
Hoofbeats of angry mules.
A wailing river.
The rain is machine gun fire.
The clamor of mothers.
Fists beating on a door.

The rain is helicopter blades.
The rain is chainsaws.
The rain is testimony.
The rain is a thousand hearts pounding.
The rain is the forest gasping.

The rain is a roll call of the dead
as Javier stands sentry with his
angel face.

Arrival
September 1960

We might crack the coconut,
we thought, by bouncing it
on the sidewalk. Those Miami palms
so tall, this day so hot: so far from Kansas,
we were starting to learn south.
Chrissie's new front teeth
showed when she laughed. Later,
fresh-braided, we clambered
onto a plane and watched
propellers shove us through a storm.
Lightning convulsed the night,
our kitten bodies restless and rooting—
at last I slept, awaking
to climb down wheeled stairs
into the viscous air of Cali: adobe arches,
tiled roofs, horns and motors, horse carts,
fountains. I tasted banana ice cream
and gave the cone to a lame beggar
who flailed and cried out,
"¡*Limosna!* For love of the Virgin,
help me!" It was translated for me,
this first ardent shout, a language
that would become mine with its heat,
succulence, entreaties,
its rainstorms and terrible hunger.

Seis
Pasto, Nariño, age six

In the balcony house, strange
sounds come from people's mouths,
their moving lips shape noises
like chocolate, like pepper,
like warm rolls on a long cloth
unspooling easily all
the way to the city's edge.
I want to catch hold, to eat
from that cloth, fling out such sounds
from the balcony rail, like Évila
calling to her brother on the patio.
And slowly I pluck
words from this moving feast,
my ears clumsy, snatching
pelota ball, *mujeres* women,
muchacho boy, *pan* bread, *rojo* red,
azúcar sugar, the cloth unrolls
and I am on it, I tumble
with *perro* dog, *cantemos* let's sing,
yo soy I am, *no llores* don't cry.

EUCALYPTUS

Wherever I go, it may ambush me:
sharp fragrance brought by who knows whom
from green New Zealand who knows when
to low green Andes of Nariño to be planted
like poetry along roads that spoke
their curves without haste. All eucalyptus
makes me seven years old, eating
an empanada stuffed with steaming pork
and potatoes, or swing-pumping myself high,
or caught in a backseat sister-squabble
and withered by Dad's rebuke with its dark overtones
of civilization itself at stake.
This bark, these leaves layer other odors: cacao
and coffee, beef and earth of Wednesday market,
the Inga people's secrets woven into blankets.
Rhymes that chimed under my scalp, Mercedes
with her *sí señora* mop, Galeras oozing concealed lava,
the scrawny baby we fed with an eyedropper
and named brother—dream tree
pungent of everything.

Maternal Gestures

Her hands moved like steel prongs
as she poured water over my bent head;
her fingers worked up lather,
swiftly rubbed my scalp,
again poured, holding
my aching neck like a vise.
Lifting my head at last,
she pulled a plastic brush
through the wet ropes.

Mom once worked a bean
out of Danny's nose with the tines of a fork.
She clamped damp shirts to lines
with staccato motions, thrust
an iron across them later
as if some deep recess harbored
a clenched coal of vengeance.

When we went to the river
her bare feet looked surprised,
so white, impossibly narrow.
As she pulled my hair
into quick braids for swimming,
I looked down, saw
her toes in a fumble of sand
like shy young girls.

Arithmetic

you are folded inside the dark little house the one where the neighbors have scratched a hole in your parents' bedroom wall to check on the doings of these tall gringos and your sweet Snowball has died after eating meat poisoned for rats and your parents are working in the dining room (Dad hammering) but mostly they are shooting each other with sharp-hooked words and the air lies on you helpless and damp as a sick baby and you are supposed to be studying but how do you practice long division when your mother is saying *You have been talking about divorce since the first year we were married* and your stomach is cramped into a burning knob and you want to shout *stop! stop!* because it is afternoon but these walls let in no light you are all strangers here and this is a kind of long division you don't know how to do

Inheritance

I inherited a path
between back door and outhouse,
a book smuggled under my shirt.
The fresh-cut wood that to myopic
eyes appeared soft, unsure,
resolved to sharp edges under
a cautious hand. I held
the book close, tucked pain
into its neat ravine as I chased words
like fishes down page-rivers,
strung them on lines. Sentences
snaked into my mind
as the tropical evening faded;
thoughts scuttled out of shadows,
climbed my legs like red ants.

      I was given
a thick obsession with words and, when
darkness had put an end to reading,
an open door and
the heartstopping light of stars
pouring silence into my squinting eyes.

Ride
Tayrona National Park, 2008

Though the sky has collapsed in overwrought theatrics,
upends great tanks of tears and cannot catch its breath,
though the path crazy-switches through rock-stubbed foothills,
lurches down bouldered ravines, slumps stone-faced, then
crumples into mud; though you,

not a practiced rider, wear a bulging bedraggled pack
and in its depths your notebooked poems may well
be washing into ink-run oblivion,

                                          you loosen the reins.
The creature under your legs' curve—intelligence
of ribs and lungs and shining hide, and hooves'
sure memory—finds her way.

                                  The sky sobs its hot joy;
over the hills, the gray sea churns. "Eh-*yah!*" shouts the driver
and you laugh at the mule's sudden canter. Your drenched
and giddy body is hers.

Tongue

Tal vez
Puerto Asís, Putumayo
1964

Maybe you and I could marry.
A man had stopped me on the village road
puddled by morning rain.
A gnat ticked at my nose. The man
stood short and neat, about my height,
hair crinkled and close-trimmed, and skin
like Sello Dorado coffee, awaiting
my response.

No, I said, and probably *gracias*,
keeping my voice
as flat as my chest. *I am too young*.
My American mother had never called
a black man handsome.
My American father had built our house.
It had no balcony for serenades.

Bilingual

What is invisible
rocks her in silent waves. She walks
hallways, dials numbers, turns
a tap for running water as if
she belonged; she listens,
answers questions, traces branches
of need and desire, decides, requires

—lives hinged in a warm mouth,
a moist fecundity, music of guitars
dizzying her core, bewildered
by fabric with its smooth yielding,
wild onion's curved stem, insistence
of July wind. How to say
it? her body has become tongue,
tasting, drawing back, a long pliant
muscle of dark words.

Bilingüe

Lo invisible la mece
en ondas silenciosas. Camina
corredores, marca números, abre
el grifo para agua como si
perteneciera aquí; escucha,
contesta preguntas, traza ramos
de añoro y necesidad, decide, exige

—vive engoznada en boca cálida,
húmeda fecundidad, música de guitarras
aturdiendo su ser, perdida en confusión
por el rendir liso de telas, tallo
encorvado de cebolla silvestre, insistencia
de un viento de julio. ¿Cómo
decirlo? su cuerpo se ha hecho lengua,
saboreando, retirándose, músculo
largo, plegable, de palabras oscuras.

FOR EXAMPLE
Apartadó, 2004

There was the boy who was torched
for refusing to join the paramilitaries.

There was his *tinto* skin
in a white-owned town, there was
his dogged effort to finish high school,
there was no job.
There was his father's flashing eye,
cross-country move to protect
the boy, there were city gangs,
addicts, no jobs.

There was the pronouncement: No son
of mine will go with *esos señores*,
those gentlemen—with careful irony—
whether sidewalk hoodlums or squads
cleansing streets with machetes
and bullets. For them, no job
too bloody, too brutal.

There was the return to Apartadó:
*At least there are friends here, we'll
keep your profile low.* One week
later, the boy was tied to a tree,
doused with gasoline, lit.

There were no rescuing police
or soldiers. No boss to note
unexplained absence the next day.
There was no prosecution;
all witnesses' reports were lost.

There was a father in desperate,
perspiring search. There were children
drawn to the blaze on that hot night,
uncomprehending,
there were cries of the damned,
a young man melting,
the smell of roasting human flesh,
smoke rising in an outraged pillar.

There were ashes on the wind for days,
gritty and restless like a father's grief.

Coco
in memory of Marino López
Cacarica, Chocó, 1997

Such a strong young man
and the coconut palm

Climb, climb now, bring
us a coconut

Round and rough and such
cool milk   —his head

So round, like a coconut
a fútbol

On this hot day
a sharp machete

Red milk, hot milk, kick

a fútbol

Now you see

NUMBERS
The accounting of Francisco Villalba, paramilitary

At Farm Thirty-Five
there were three covered trucks.
Twenty-five of us were in training,
we rose at five a.m.
Three times I was called
to take part in cutting.
I stood guard twice,
I cut once. She was young,
she said she had two children.
Four hundred are buried now.
I took one arm.

A FORMER SERGEANT EXPLAINS
LAS LISTAS DE EXTERMINACIÓN

After all, it was proved
and meticulously cross-checked:
each one was a collaborator.

Presidential qualities

El presidente, Harvard graduate,
fervent servant of the North,
privatizes with panache—water,
power, telephone company,
universities to the highest bidder.

In Washington *el presidente*
agrees to everything—having paid
PR companies to teach
Washington what to require.
Every three months, in superb synchrony,
Post, *Times*, *Tribune* editorialize
el presidente's praise.

In his capital *el presidente*
scolds his people: small farmers
hounded off their land, and all those
defending them, are terrorists,
those denouncing him insurgents, but
those who bought votes the nation's martyrs.

What is a constitution?
Only a rag of history on which
a president's nose might be blown.
What is justice? A mat
for wiping *el presidente*'s feet.
Our benefactors? You will
know them by their Northern names:
Occidental, Drummond, Coca-Cola,
taking our oil and coal, selling us
obese refreshment.

Who are the poor? The good ones—
those who eat with quiet mouths,
who shake their hips and laugh for tourists,
who vote for *el presidente* and then
go back to cleaning his palace,
who never raise signs in the plaza.

So white is *el presidente*, like
a bleached-flour *arepa* or a sheet of paper,
he and Washington on the same page.
How dry he is, untropical,

desiccated as rainforest land
under the palm plantations,
dry as the bones buried deep
in fields of paramilitary friends,
parched white bones of the disappeared.

Ashore
Curvaradó, Chocó
in memory of Orlando Valencia, October 2005

The morning after her father's
body was identified, Leidy
awoke and asked for rice,
a fried plantain. There was
no oil for frying. Chewing
her rice, she pushed away
her brother's swinging foot,
swatted at gnats, pressed
against her mother's silent bulk.
Next she would ask for cheese,
a square of salty white *quesito*,
and then—

                He had raged
against the killings, desecration
of land with canals, plantations,
false titles. His eyes flamed, words
burned, he was a torch.

Police stopped him on the way
to an election; they let him go and
the paramilitaries came.

The river seemed relieved
to give him up: he surfaced near
Chigorodó, a bloated mass, facedown,
nudging a canoe as if knocking
absently at a door. He was hauled
ashore, wrapped gingerly in plastic.
They took fingerprints, sent for his wife

to view the face marred by blows
and decomposing, the puckered forehead
bullet hole—she glanced,
shuddered, nodded, turned away.

                Leidy stood
by the breakfast fire and stretched.
She would ask to swim, she decided,
and then she'd ask for a stalk
of cane. She was big enough
to peel one with quick machete strokes.
She would string wants
across this damp, unnaturally quiet day,
she would take aim with words,
she would keep asking.

NIGHTS, DAYS
for Ingrid Betancourt, 2008

The rough hands. The blindfold.
Green shadows when it is pulled off.
The shouts. The starchy boiled plantains.
The forced marches. The sweat.
Clara's voice in the night, *Ay. Ay. No.*
The black ants. The climbing.
The shouts. The rough hands.
The radio static. The camera.
My mouth uttering taught words.
The starchy boiled plantains. The rice.
The nightmares of suffocation.
Swelling of Clara's belly. The nights.
The days of sweat. The shouts.
The threats. My sticky arms
against my body. Lorenzo
in my thoughts. Clara's wails,
her pale child squinting. Melanie.
The radio static. The nights.
Fungus mapping lost nations
on my skin. The starchy boiled plantains.
The cookfires. The smoke.
The threats. The sluggish river.
The forced marches. The shouts.
My sticky arms against my body.
Melanie. My mouth. The rice. Lorenzo.
The climb. The helicopter.
                                     The sudden.
What I've carried in the womb,
what will be born.

Perancho
after Eduardo Galeano and Raúl Zurita

Death is raining, says Galeano,
along the Perancho and Peranchito.
My love in the river's silt,
among *cativo* stumps: *llueve muerte*.
La Llorona's tears drift over us
mixed with ashes of burning forests.
Where will the sloth live?
My love in the dead groves, beyond
the murderous palms: I wanted you
without poison, I wanted you starry
with milk and pendulous leaves.

Color of Earth

SYLLOGISM
Chocó, 2003

Under a pressing sun
you live damp amid
damp trees, steaming
green weight of forest
veined with rivers, your back
with trails of sweat, eyes
craving the austerity of rocks,
nails permanently grimed,
words either fierce
or exhausted:

but *quícharo* fish
lies on your plate like salted
angel's wings
and *tacana* braids
succulent red blooms through
sloping branches
and papaya parted
to give its dripping flesh
smells like hallelujah

and every night secrets
circle candles like moths,
amazement alights
on windows, downy
as a small brown bat

and the exaltation of downpours—
no wonder children splash and leap,
no wonder the river.

Nueva Vida chirimía
CAVIDA, a community of resistance
Chocó

Clarinet bounces like girls
at *fútbol*, like dogs in river play;
accordion stitches our land's
wide boundaries, and scraper
pulses a man planting corn,
women laundering, boys
shouting times tables.
We shine, children of Africa, and mourn
chopper blades, machine gun fire,
a war that is not ours, that slashes
at bones   skin   branches,
that burns our houses and our fields.
That took Marino's cresting laughter,
Manuela's spirit stories, Jairo's limp,
and many others. We answer
with music, insist on rice
and *yuca*, fried *boquiancha*,
guinea's blooms blazing like prayers,
the coolness of thatched roofs,
machetes for peeling cane
and opening paths. Baths
in the Perancho, women ripening
with children who will not go hungry.

BRAIDS
CAVIDA, 2003

On the ground, Esperanza holds Fanny
    between her long straight legs,
        clips thin *gajitos* with barrettes.
            (This land fastens us
            to its pulsing skin.)

        Deft comb and fingers part Anita's hair
in swift rows, then weave head-snug *cadenitas*.
Yesenia bands her *moños*;
        Viviana's *chulitos* cascade thick
           as bean vines on a pole.

Consuelo rests her old bones while
    Anita ties a simple *moño* on her head,
        then braids a *cadenita*, then repeats
           (just like our fields,
    a row of rice, then two of corn,
and then tomatoes and papaya).

We're braided to this soil—its vines
        and stalks, its root-twined riverbanks,
      mosquitoes' needling in *cativo* groves,
butterflies, petals, *quícharo*—

        and braided each to each, we carry tanks
           in shouting teams, clear brush,
        mix herb poultices for aches.

Cookfire smoke braids river mist, our breath,
      our jokes and proclamations,
           fresh-milled fragrant hot *panela*,
      words of scripture read at dawn
           by Deya and Marcelo.

We twist and knot in argument,
    fail fevered under nets,
        loosen with laughter and shared soup,
    entangle and reknit along the ardent
        limbs of night.

PORTRAIT
CAVIDA, 2003

Across the resin table
we face each other,
chalk palette spread
like sidewalk wares.

You choose background of blue;
I ponder how to make
your brown—mahogany
or layering red and green?

You watch my fingers
shape and rub; I watch
you and find your skin's
light. The sun drifts

across you with
ineffable tenderness,
catches beads of sweat.
I am in love

with your hair's
lush mass, the gray-
pink line that rims
your witness lips.

Your hands brood
in your lap like
two doves, your eyelids
murmur names.

STUNG
Chocó, 2003

Mosquitoes and biting flies of this place
prefer white meat, your new friends joke:
your legs are their fresh banquet bars,
and so you learn the rhythmic towel
leg-swatting that might mitigate
the map of dots and welts that throng
across your shins and ankles now,
district of angry villages, deranged
itch for friction, nail claw-sharpness,
pink profusion, seven daft demons,
you an addled magdalene.

ECOSYSTEM
Chocó, 2003

Under the mosquito net I slope
toward sleep's gray sea
and howler monkeys pose
dark questions and the mice
commence their circuits
along the tops of walls and frogs chirp
in the swamp for mates and suddenly
my bed begins to rock, the house to creak
on its low posts, the floor beams just
beneath me heave—and then come grunts
and snuffles: a wayfaring
sow has scratched
her back to satisfaction.

INCURSION
Jiguamiandó River Basin, Chocó
March 3, 2003

"We are here to *protect* civilians"—
the commander spreads complaints
with a wide spoon.
"We're tired of the guerrillas' slick disguises,
dressing up like us, United Self-Defense,
to blow up bridges, commit barbarities."
His eyes tighten. "¿Comprende usted?"

Afternoon haze settles
across his cheekbones; he folds
his arms, silently questions my pale skin,
braids and cotton shorts: a gringa tourist
in this jungle?

Yes, I wish to say—thanks
to the villagers. It was your men
who shot Hermín, age eleven,
fishing with his father, left him dead.
Your Self-Defense troops
stopped Aníbal just last week
as he collected firewood; later
at your base, he was interrogated,
pummeled, killed. Are *you* guerrillas, then,
decked out as Self-Defense?

We stand between wincing river
and schoolhouse shelter, where
another man in camouflage taunts
huddled villagers: "Wouldn't you like
to wear a Self-Defense armband?"
Someone's parrot, assuming a party,

cackles giddily from a roof beam.
Ermenson, thirteen, brother to Hermín
and witness, leans on his mother, shaking.
For days he has scarcely spoken.

And my own mouth is dry, deserted
by all words but one. I nod
to the commander and say "Sí," by which
both of us realize I mean *No*.

Sabbath
CAVIDA, 2003

The women in the Adventist church
shine beside their menfolk: pastel green
and blue dresses, white collars.
Two men wear ties. Children lean
on parents, stare at feet in unaccustomed
sandals. This is the earnest church,
not like the Pentecostal with its clamor.
Here God is addressed soberly, following
a lesson plan's numbered points. Leaders
step from behind a panel one by one
to read an exhortation, launch a hymn,
urge us toward truth.

                        Having failed
to inquire, I've arrived underdressed
in shorts and a loose shirt. A hymnbook
is shared; I hum into each song,
finding the alto.

For Sabbath school, outdoors,
adults set chairs in a wide circle.
Our leader, the young schoolteacher,
cycles us through texts on prayer.
Toward the end, I ask about forgiveness.

He understands. We can pray,
he says, for our enemies' conversion.
When Saul raged against and killed
the early Christians, some of them
must have prayed for him.

Is it easy or hard? I ask.
We are thinking of our dead.
The man next to me smiles, says
it's easy if you stay close to God.
The teacher probes: Hard
for human beings, very hard, but God
gives us *poder*—capacity.

Conversations erupt around the circle
—what can we forgive? does forgiving
mean forgetting?
                                  Where will prayer
take us? Into our pain, insistence
that God be with us in throbbing
of helicopter blades and anxious hearts.

Planting Our Names

Under

I return to passion fruit, to patios,
bees hovering in geraniums,
muted voices, small girls tossing silky hair
over their shoulders like wind bending grasses.
To clouds, swimming strokes, water
pouring itself, pouring.

I write about death
and pull back: how to approach
without saying *dead, blood, body*
or *murderous intent*, without saying *Colombia*,
paramilitary or *gun*. Only the sweat
on people's lips, the bus's lumbering trajectory,
the bags of beans and corn, the sleeping child,
the checkpoint, selection of passengers,
chainsaw's sharp-toothed snarl.

The river passes, keeps passing, folding itself
around this bend, accepts and folds in
two long bags weighted with stones.
They slide to its muddy depths, the river
rises imperceptibly, returns to its pastime
of folding to catch sun fragments:
Catch. Mirror. Flash. Fold.

NEW STONES
Peace Community of San José de Apartadó, Antioquia
February 21, 2005

"We are defenders of life and of the dignity of persons."
—Luis Eduardo Guerra, community founder

The day is ordinary, hot;
Deiner, age eleven, trudges
beside his father, carries burlap bags,
machete to clear brush around cacao trees.
Luis Eduardo pulls a shirttail up to wipe
his neck. Deiner keeps close: the son
of one who speaks for the community,
designs its rules for peace (no service
to armed factions, not even selling food),
who flies to Amsterdam,
Chicago and Fort Benning—this son
will always wish for more.
More days like this, sun burning
through clouds, long plantain leaves
angling over path. Deiner whistles,
jokes with father and stepmother,
watches for snakes.

When they spot an armed man, Luis
shoots a warning glance, steps forward.
A dozen more emerge from the trees:
then it is thudding blows
insults and hoarse wails

rifle prod in back
forced stumbling march

and Deiner's father cannot shield him.

Later, at Mulatos River, an egret
catches the boy's dazed eyes: white
amid green shadows on the far bank,
gathering its strength to rise in flight
through and above the trees.

Now you may need to turn the page.

For if you stay, and travel with the search party,
at the river you will find three
entangled bodies, boy's head tossed
to one side, flesh gouged by vultures.

The soldiers have long since returned
to their barracks, bathed, traded wisecracks.
The peace community mourns,
rages, calls for a reckoning, adds
three stones to its memorial, risen to
one hundred fifty-four.
Generals deny, ministers pronounce,
diplomats listen with grave faces.

Clouds over San José gather
and disperse, the sky shimmers,
wears its impassive gleam as
unbearable words dig into paper,
piercing our skin and muscles,
hollow a space for harsh
remembering, a poem
for the violence of peace.

SHRINE
for ASFADDES,
Association of Relatives
of the Detained and Disappeared
Medellín

Libia has left Angel's briefs
and shirts in the bottom dresser drawer.
She is used to waking up alone
now, eating her *arepa* with the radio
for company. The corner store
where she sells pastries and coffee
is populated with neighbors,
and when her daughter calls—
Angel's daughter—
she holds the phone carefully
like a rosary or a
loaded gun.

Six years ago
she propped an Angel photo
inside the front-hall recess
next to the Virgin's white skirts.
Coming and going, Libia brushes
fingers against them both.

It was dangerous to be a Quintero:
over the years eight of Angel's clan—
uncles, cousins, brother—
had vanished. Police
detained them, filed
no record of arrest. At protests
he cried out their names,
and to the high commissioner.

Families of the disappeared
are family to each other, holding
each other's daily emptiness—one
October night in a restaurant,
with *sancocho* and dark jokes.
Leaving with Claudia to see her home,
Angel flashed his smile, hugged everyone.
A white car stopped, they
were snatched by shadows.

If he comes back, says Libia, he will need
these shoes.

GEOGRAPHY OF A SAINT
for Piedad

I would paint you enormous,
a Fernando Botero woman
with boulders for arms
and hair like Tequendama Falls.

Your heart is a mountain
around whose peak clouds
tear themselves in shreds.
I would paint you clutching
bouquets of trees, crimping
the edges of the world
like petticoats in your fists.

Your prayers emerge in gusts; you lean
crosslegged toward the sea.
Jesus crouches with you, bleeds
and rocks in your shadow,
small as a stone.
Reaching, you pull down the sky
to wrap around the two of you
like a shawl whose fringe
catches in the foam of ebbing tide.

Family stories
for the Nasa people, Northern Cauca

If you ask our elders, they will
tell you: Little sister,
our Mother grieves.
Convulsions of the sky:
listen.
The wounding of forests:
listen.
Creatures estranged
from soil: listen.

Take time, little sister,
to hear our Mother's stories.
They are full of beetles,
mold and mountains,
the busyness of birds.
Roots twist through her stories;
in the telling she rests.
We are created,
we are not alone.

With the ocean's waves
our Mother's heartbeat rocks us.
We soothe her by listening,
by tending her streams.

Tonight I will write a poem.
Tomorrow I will lean against a tree
and listen.

*   *   *

I dreamed Juan Tama, the sacred lake
high up the snow-capped Huila.
I dreamed a meeting of our peoples.

Rodolfo, peace pastor, walks
smiling, reads the earth
with Mayan eyes as lakewater
laps his brown feet,
clear as a dream.

Las horas del corazón
Quibdó, 2014

Midnight, and under the mosquito net
your mattress, the familiar lumps.
The air presses its hot blanket
over you, but thunder
has growled an end to the dance music
across the ravine, and now the rain, *un aguacero*,
starts to tap a rapid beat.

¿Qué horas son? The hours
of the heart, the dark hours,
grasping the cords
of memory—river baths,
the long boats carrying *plátanos*,
strangers smoking in the plaza,
your brother's blood that wrote
its own rivers on the floor—
las horas que no se van because
they grip you and will not stop speaking.

Ayer

Comes las horas, masticas
lentamente. Ayer en la lluvia
las máquinas lloraban,
y en los periódicos, columnas
de letras débiles. Todo
lo cargas en la mandíbula,
la barriga: historia
de puñetazos, cuchillo.
La niña en el río.
Tres jóvenes encendidos.
Tus manos susurran,
hojas de un libro terco.

Yesterday

You eat your hours, chewing
without haste. Yesterday in the rain
the machines wept,
and in the newspapers, columns
of feeble letters. You carry it all
in your jaw, your belly:
history of blows, a knife.
The girl in the river.
Three boys on fire.
Your hands speak softly,
leaves of a stubborn book.

Testigo
para Marino Córdoba

Desde aquí vas al río acongojado,
corrientes de tristeza que visitas
a diario, amigo fiel de aguas
que alzan, lloran —color de tierra
brillando bajo sol incomprensivo—
que cargan la verdad en sus entrañas.
Junto al río te paras,
un árbol recto y completo en tu silencio.

Witness
for Marino Córdoba

From here you to go the churning river,
current of sadness you visit
daily, faithful friend of waters
that rise and lament—color of earth
shining beneath uncomprehending sun—
that carry the truth in their depths.
By the river you stand like a tree,
upright and perfect in your silence.

Our voices, our hands

With baskets of rice and plantains
from the market, with bulging bags
of potatoes, with happiness creasing
their faces, people lined up long
to vote. Each mother,
when it came time to cast her ballot, passed
her baby to a neighbor. For babies
it was a day of hot damp arms, new smells
in cotton stretched over the landscape of chest
and shoulder, a different voice vibrating
the neck.
                That was the day
Gloria became mayor of Apartadó
and the next morning was born pink
and unbearably soft at the east horizon.

*   *   *

The prayer meeting convenes
after nightfall, twelve people crowded
into one room, on stools and the hard floor,
two candles and a flashlight to illumine
the word of God. Voices join
in simultaneous supplication,
Sofía's strongest, surging
through pleas and praises
like an urgent river.

*   *   *

Sara is whipping her three-
year-old son. "Stay on your knees!"
she shouts. "Stop crying!"

He does not know how to stop,
his mouth stretches wide, a permanent
wail, no! no! He runs and falls,
she follows, lashes, calls him
disgraced, misbegotten; screams
and the leather strap's broad *whap!*
whap! confuse the air, we all recoil,
cringe, beg, we are all screaming.

*   *   *

It was downriver, said Inés—the *paras*
came with their shouts and their rifles,
they said no more shit,
you have to go. They took my man
and never gave him back. I ran,
our child inside me, through the trees
and the cleared fields. The leaves,
I do not know if they pitied me,
I ran gasping and clutched my stomach
and they were green, green.

*   *   *

In the peace
of another day, Deya leaves work
and goes to visit Sara. Perching her bulk
on the porch's edge, stout legs
swinging, she chats and smiles
into the distance. She saves
her neighbor's life, saying:
We do not need to beat our children.
We can talk to them instead.

Our parents thought we would grow wild
if they did not whip us, force us
to kneel, be silent. I remember,
but it is not so.
You're a good mother, Sara.
We do not need to whip our children.

*   *   *

When I was detained, Margarita said,
there were dozens in jail and I sat
alone, weeping, in a stubble of murmurs
and fearful perspiration. Then a roar
began to grow, distant like thunder
or a strange machine. Louder and
louder, it swelled into my name,
chanted. I stood up, wiped my cheeks.

Outside, they tell me, women
had arrived in black, one hundred
or so, circling the jail. They lit
candles and moved about in rituals,
cleansing the place. Police, terrified
of witches, pulled back. My sisters
chanted my name and others'.
Officers came for us, befuddled,
led us through halls
and shadows, out to voices
planting our names like seeds.

What Our Mother Taught Us

Soap is political

say the Cacarica women. We
would like to make our own.

They teach me river laundering:
Prop board on stool in shallow water
and straddle. Swirl your garment
in the slow current. Soft brown creatures
like tadpoles, nudging your shins,
won't bite. Rub the blue soap bar
across the shirt, both sides,
take a brush and scrub. Put your weight
into it, lean and press
as if cleansing six years' pain.
Rinse, again swirling. Raise
this paddle, wad your shirt, strike it,
turn, and pound. Twist now from both ends,
lay in your basin to hang-dry later.

Laundry on the river ebbs
and flows with gossip,
rhythm of paddling, laughter,
specks of soapy spray. Some women
wash for a household of ten.
We like our clothes immaculate,
they say, but try to be frugal with soap.
Too much will harm our fish.

Last year we learned a recipe
for soap, the best so far, but one
ingredient must be bought:
sodium carbonate. If we shipped in
quantities, they'd jump to say
it's for processing coca.
We don't need more accusations.

Remember, then, when you visit
Cacarica: soap is the best gift.

Chocó, January 2003

Excavation
Colombia–Chicago

That last week at home I chewed
inside my cheek—salt stung
almost unbearably.

Once here, I wore a coat
every day for months,
sticking my arms into puffs
of pillowed fabric and moving
down cold streets, detached
as the Virgin of Las Lajas.

For six months I also wore a smile
but now sometimes my skin collapses.
The consul is collecting names.

My welcomers found a car for me.
They do not remember
that in my country gravel
under the pipeline is mixed
with shards of human bone.

My dreams are still full
of ants and wasps,
country buses with rice bags
and chickens and room for one more
perspiring human. Helicopters,
girls waving white towels.
I always visit the same office
crowded with certificates:
an oily man says all is well,
we have put down the disturbance.

There is a miner in my brain
prodding deep strata with a pick.
My mother's forearm
emerges like a vein of coal,
steady and dark, resting after laundry
against her stomach. I twist
myself in her skirts.

Asilo means refuge
but in my new language it is *asylum*.

Beholding

Stars in Putumayo nights pressed
toward my face, eager as beggars.
The dark was filled with light; earth
and sky leaned humidly against each other
like lovers thick with thoughts. My book
of Greek-named constellations was too pale
and decorous for such a burgeoning:
I drank stars with my eyes, swallowed
their burning night after night.

                      That first year
neighbor children crowded to peer
daily through our screen door, amazed
by our light hair, the time we spent with books,
our alien tongues. In their world we
were reluctant stars, appearing unbidden,
strange and populous, full of secrets.

Your face holds light along cheekbones,
eyebrow ridges, the curve around each nostril.
What possessed me to think
I could lean on this door frame, enter
your gaze, be held in your seeing?
I burn blindly in shadows, outcrying:
O have mercy, we are found and lost again, O
your shoulders, your tongue, your stars.

After you

Now that you are gone, I wipe
mango juice from my table,
fold up the crinkled stories

Three potatoes on the windowsill
begin to send out roots
from their sleeping eyes

I dream that I begin to travel
but the moon stops me, flicking
its bright coins against my mirror

Poems litter the path
where we walked, and all my clothes
are stained with your laughter

La Niña
"It has never rained so much in Colombia."
—Guardian Weekly, *May 10, 2011*

In the earth of my skin, in its ashes,
the guitar of me is strummed
for tired songs. Above us clouds bulge,
balloon, collapse into torrents,
and mountainsides, logged
and grazed to nakedness,
slump into ruin over homes
and paths. Stones lie bewildered,
guava trees plucked like weeds
rot in a tangle of branches.

In the earth of my skin this lament,
my peasant bones cry *madre mía*,
how we have confounded your calm,
how we have bruised you, our Mother.

This war
USA

This war folds us tightly
in its deepest pocket.
We are caught in creases of rayon:
here it is hard to breathe.
Our shoes with their knife heels
take down Brazilian forests.
Our children learn to torture.
We buy chocolate for comfort,
weep for the slave boys
on Sierra Leone plantations.

This war is about weather:
a glacier of ice coats our alley in March
like a long scar, while at the equator
its cousin the ocean forces up the skirts
of a twitching island nation.

This war is called Extraction.
It is fought on television,
the painted sides of trains,
in space, rainforests, boardrooms,
human minds. It smells of cheese
and, elsewhere, gasoline.
Its secret name is Hunger
and Exile.

One front erupts
on a dark Colombian morning
as boats roar up the river and stop
to disgorge men dressed in camouflage.
Go to your Maker, insurgent! Omar,
a high school teacher, pulled from bed

shirtless and blinking,
falls like sugarcane
under machete's blow,
one of many, a great harvest
of teeth, blood,
                    land, and this is what
Riosucio has to do with Richmond,
Chocó with Chicago: this land
with its abundant water, its great trees,
is now declared vacant,
planted with oil palms
that feed on Omar's decomposing limbs
and all the others',
and are processed into biofuel.
In my garage
on a cold Chicago morning
I start my car, I don't want to know
about Omar or his land.

This war is planted in orderly rows.
It has green asparagus fingernails
and drinks bottled water.
It is well manicured
and often wears the Organic label.
We need to bomb many villages
in order to save them
with gene-perfected seeds
so they will forever depend on us
and learn to worship our god Market.

This war pumps oil ferociously,
pausing for no sabbath,
no Easter. Nuclear plants swallow
their own terrifying waste
with a calculated casual air,
like María shielding cocaine pellets
in her distended belly, mule to Miami.

This war digs in its talons
with hot sweet drinks in paper cups.
This war scratches every itch,
indulges whims, strikes down laws,
encases everything in molded plastic.

This war is engorged with bananas,
wide streets and garbage.
It gulps and digests human lives,
bulldozes shacks of the poor,
computerizes, lays off,
puts a knife to the neck of rivers.
It is self served, sweat shopped,
antibacterial, asthmatic,
deep dished, hypertense,
super sized, commodity traded,
cancer formed, cash cropped.

We bow before you, Market.
We give ourselves to you,
we bring our children to your altar
and all the world's brown people
who had been lost without you.
We build you shrines in Baghdad,
Beijing, Bogotá: for your glory
we light eternal fires.

Judith tells me stories

Por acá los alambres, la fosa
a este lado. A nature preserve
once they excavate the bones. Oh Medellín,
what an undertaking. Get your shelves
ready, your tweezers, *palas, limas.*

Andrés went out to get bread for his mother.
Genoveva heard the shots and said, *¡Andrés!*
Jota jumped up, whining at the door.
We couldn't leave the boy there, blood-slumped
over the curb. The bread was mashed.
Las palomas comieron pan.

We're the world's happiest people
aunque tenemos tantos muertos.
Así aguantamos. Fabiola waits
for her reparations check.
Luis was gunned down on a corner.
Mi hijo, mi pobre hijo. She hasn't found
her way to happiness yet,
she probably never will. Some of us
are not so strong.

When your father invited me to work
in the city, my father said no,
I was just fifteen, too young to go so far.
I had packed just in case,
three dresses and a pair of shoes
in a cardboard box. Don Pablo
returned to the truck, Martha beside him.

Papá, quiero ir, I begged. *Por fin
dijo que sí*; I ran out shouting,
¡Esperen, esperen! They stopped,
I went in for the box, and we took off.

All those years of working, fifteen
with your parents, then garment factories
—I always loved machines. My girls
and their cousins took care of each other;
we left them food each day.

Once I told your mother,
Hay que soltar la rabia.
Most beautiful city, Medellín:
come stay next time you visit,
see how the light falls
in the apartment Isabel bought me,
the potted palm old Jota nearly killed
has grown back,
see the green fan of its fronds.

What Our Mother Taught Us

In the rattling red Jeep that crept
the road-ribbon's pinched
descent from Pasto to Putumayo lowlands,
edged with sharp dropoff,
sheer green and tumbled boulders,
through the fog-breath of mountains
past tipsy crosses, so many,
proclaiming that when a landslide
shoves us over the edge of the world,
when a bus careens off a precipice and crushes
those we love most, God
falls too
                          —our songs kept us
fastened to our seats and to each other
over the river and through the woods,
where *this old man*
came rolling home. And we did too.

* * *

Our mother sang with us at bedtime,
a hug around the neck
and a barrel and a heap,
our father at any moment,
with finger upraised, *for a duck*
may be somebody's brother.

At night in church in Puerto Asís
with no music on the pages, only words,
no light but candles,
no instruments but voices,
¡Aleluya, te alabamos!

For flashlight-lit walks
to the Villa Garzón outhouse, where
coral snakes might stretch across the path
like bead necklaces carelessly dropped,
my sisters told me to sing Psalm 23—
junto a él caminaré, en su brazo confiaré,
nada del amor de Dios me apartará.
I tried it and the night folded in
my quavering voice with frog chirrups and bat squeaks,
and the trees at the edge of our yard
whispered a thousand whirring wings.

* * *

I'd rather be a forest than a street
we sang as teens in Medellín, perched
on the porch railing with its shameless
fall of bougainvillea, above the city
hammocked between mountains,
with its engines and frothy juices, buses grumbling
odorous exhaust. Our guitars sang
the city's windows and downpours,
the electricity of its nights, its tile roofs
and printing presses,
torment of its boys' dark curls and hands.
We didn't know
the bishops were meeting in 1968
to debate gospel liberation, but we learned
Con los pobres de la tierra
quiero yo mi suerte echar, and then
Viglietti's song with its coined
unbarbedwiring: *A desalambrar, a desalambrar,*
que la tierra es nuestra y tuya y de aquel—

return the land to *Pedro, María,*
Juan y José.

My guitar rode buses into the mountains
where we would alight and tramp through fields,
make picnic near a rushing stream.
Por algún camino yo lo encontraré
—I will find him on some path, maybe
this one. Our cotton songs soaked up
este amor que descubrí en la almohada,
que me hace olvidar hasta el nombre—
and there beside the stream and its insistent rocks
we forgot our names for love.

* * *

When our mother lay dying many years later
in the grayed colors of an ER alcove
and Laura and Gilberto and I leaned close
she smiled and said, "Sing something."
We started an old heaven song,
Cuan gloriosa será la mañana
cuando venga Jesús el Salvador,
and though Gilberto's voice had ever
proved itself raucously ungovernable,
this day for Mama Susy it found the tune-path
and trod it in ecstasy for all three stanzas.
United like sisters, all our nations
will give you welcome. Mom smiled
her *barrel and a heap*
that keeps me talking in my sleep,
and her last words were to our dad, "Paul, pray,"
and then she finished breathing.

Allí llanto no habrá—no crying there, for God
will sing over us forever.

* * *

In Puerto Lleras the urgent whisper
ahí vienen—they're coming—
jolts us like a whip. The children
with whom I have been singing climb
the shelter's steps, except
a four-year-old who cannot find
her mother, so I pick her up.
And from the river, men approach
in single file, machine guns slung
over shoulders, and everything
has been said—these are civilians,
leave them alone, there are no weapons
here but those you bear—and the day
balances us on its weary back,
the river's long tongue keeps trying
to efface memories, the child
sweats against me, and now I am singing,
in English, a loud psalm: *You are
my hiding place
You always fill my heart
with songs of deliverance*
and the men's heads turn in puzzlement
and behind them, licking its banks,
the current glides. *Whenever
I am afraid I will trust in you*
and soon we will launch canoes
loaded with our clothes and tins,
our chickens, mattresses

and potted herbs, elders and babies,
move downriver to a harbor of friends
and replant our lives, and sing.

Canción de cuna
en memoria, P.M.

Porque una vez aquí estuvimos
y me contaste de tu madre,
el servicio que prestaba a muchos hombres
y tú hambrienta, oscura.
Porque una sed inmensa
quedó en ti, como el mar
no de las doradas playas
sanandresinas con turistas
y lustrosos caracoles —mas bien
de Buenaventura, puerto sucio,
hediendo a pescado y sangre.
Mujer negra, lengua salada,
arraigada en tu Colombia coja,
de noche tus carcajadas
de rebeldía nos arrullan.

Lullaby
in memory of P.M.

Because we were here together once
and you told me about your mother,
her services to many men
and you in the dark, starving.
Because a vast thirst
stayed in you, like the sea,
not the gilded beaches
of San Andrés Island with tourists
and gleaming shells, but sea
of Buenaventura, that grimy port
with its stench of fish and blood.
Black woman, tongue-salty,
lashed to your rickety Colombia,
at night your whoops
of rebel laughter bring us peace.

Extranjera

Of my heart   The shacks
kilómetro tras kilómetro
the mules, the scattering children
y qué trabajo   You sweat
the war twists your bones
so many   *en la tierra*

I came back to taste you
ajo y comino   mercados
mounds of yuca and potatoes
smelling of roots and earth
Medellín, Cali
salsa en la plaza
(*el verde tuyo*)

My stranger, I put
dedo a tu mejilla   the coarse
morning of dust
under my finger   *Aquí*

in this again rain
*en el mar de petróleo   tantos
en las bananeras*

or in the city hanging
on the ledge of a mountain
en cada esquina
your acrobatic boys

Ay mi amor   how we estrange
each other   *pobres de paciencia*
I am trying to read what
you write on me: *necesidad*

The war forks our tongues
ay mi amor   it ruins
all our plantings

Come close
smell my wrists, my neck
centímetro tras centímetro
de mis olores   tus colores
Find something true
Wayúu women claiming
their land by the sea
piedras de memoria

Plant something in me
algunas hierbas   passionfruit
a book of songs

Voy contigo, amor cansado
digamos, digamos algo nuevo
(I am not leaving)

Glossary

Only names and terms not explicitly defined in their context are included here.

acompañante. One who accompanies; used for international persons who live and work alongside Colombian communities and leaders to give witness and safety in presence.

actores armados. Armed actors—a term applied to the various armed groups involved in Colombia's long-running civil conflict.

ajo y comino. Garlic and cumin.

algunas hierbas. Some herbs (or grasses).

ametralladora. Machine gun.

Apartadó. Town in Antioquia Department in northern Colombia.

aquí. Here.

arepa. Corn cake.

arroz con pollo. Rice with chicken, a pilaf that is common in many Latin American countries.

así aguantamos. That's how we keep going.

aunque tenemos tantos muertos. Although we have so many dead.

barrio. Urban neighborhood.

Betancourt, Ingrid. A French-Colombian senator and presidential candidate who was kidnapped by the leftist FARC in 2002 and rescued by government forces, along with several other hostages, in 2008.

boquiancha. A native river fish, *Gilbertolus alatus*.

centímetro tras centímetro / de mis olores, tus colores. Centimeter by centimeter / of my odors, your colors.

chirimía. Band music of various genres, typical of Afro-Colombian culture in Chocó Department and south along the Pacific coast.

chirimoya. South American fruit called cherimoya or custard apple in English.

¿Comprende usted? Do you understand?

comunidad de resistencia, comunidad de paz. Grassroots communities seeking to stay out of Colombia's war often call themselves communities of resistance or peace communities.

Córdoba, Marino. Chocó native, founder of AFRODES (Association of Displaced Afro-Colombians); won US political asylum because of numerous attacks and death threats.

cuaderno. School notebook, traditionally stapled (saddle stitched) rather than bound with a wire spiral.

cuy. Guinea pig, traditionally raised as a source of meat among indigenous people in southern Colombia.

dedo a tu mejilla. Finger to your cheek.

denunciar. To denounce—here, to report a political murder or another violation of human rights.

desaparecido. Person who has been disappeared—detained secretly, usually by agents of the state. The vast majority of the disappeared are never heard from again.

descuartizar. To dismember.

desplazada. Person who has been forcibly displaced from her home and land.

el verde tuyo. Your green.

en cada esquina. On every corner.

en el mar de petróleo, tantos / en las bananeras. In the sea of petroleum, so many / in the banana plantations.

en la tierra. In the earth/ground (that is, buried).

Esperen. Wait (imperative).

este amor que descubrí en la almohada. This love I discovered on my pillow (phrase from "Este amor" by the Argentinian singer Piero).

extranjera. Foreigner.

fútbol. Soccer.

glifosato. Broad-spectrum herbicide, active ingredient in a potent version of Monsanto's Roundup weed killer that is used for aerial fumigation of coca plants.

guinea. Local name for a tall, upright flowering plant in Chocó rainforests.

Hay que soltar la rabia. You must let go of anger.

insurgente. Insurgent, a term applied to members of left-wing guerrilla forces.

las horas del corazón. The time of the heart.

Las palomas comieron pan. The pigeons ate bread.

limas. Metal files.

limosna. Alms.

los mochas. Those who chop off; local slang for Colombian paramilitaries.

mi pobre hijo. My poor son.

movilizar. To mobilize, generally for protests/demonstrations.

pala. Shovel.

Papá, quiero ir. Daddy, I want to go.

Perancho, Peranchito. Rivers in the Cacarica River Basin, which empties into the great Atrato River, Chocó.

paramilitar. Member of a right-wing paramilitary group. Often these groups have worked closely with the Colombian armed forces. The largest groups were officially disbanded/demobilized in 2003–4, but they reorganized under new names and have continued to wreak brutality in many parts of the country.

piedras de memoria. Stones of memory.

pobres de paciencia. Patience-impoverished.

Por acá los alambres, la fosa a este lado. The wires [wire fencing] over here, the [mass] grave on this side.

Por fin dijo que sí. At last he said yes.

puta. Prostitute; a highly derogatory term.

¿Qué horas son? What time is it?

quícharo. A native river fish, *Hoplias malabaricus*.

requisar. To expropriate (a building, a vehicle, food, etc.) for use by an armed group.

sancocho. Home-style soup with any kind of meat (chicken, fish, pork, or beef), *yuca*, potato, plantain, and other vegetables.

tal vez. Perhaps.

vallenato. Folk/pop music style from Colombia's Caribbean coast, typically using accordion along with other instruments.

Voy contigo, amor cansado / digamos, digamos algo nuevo. I'm going with you, tired love / let's say, let's say something new.

yuca. Cassava or manioc, a tuberous root vegetable.

Acknowledgments

How grateful I am to my parents, Susy and Paul Goring, who moved our family to Colombia before they'd even learned the language, teaching us by example that love is a risk worth taking.

My sisters and brothers (Christine, Martha, Mary Beth, Tim, Dan, Jen, Esther) are my dearest friends and have laughed and cried over my poems. I thank them, along with my children, Claire Márquez and Graham Stewart, my daughter-in-law Kate Stewart, and my luminous granddaughter Bea. You always inspire me.

In Colombia my gratitude and respect extend to more people than I can name. *Gracias especiales* to Luz Marina Becerra Panesso, Noelia Moya, Ana Gloria Cañizales, Silvia Rodriguez, and others of AFRODES (particularly its founder, Marino Córdoba) and the Coordinación Nacional de Mujeres Afrocolombianas Víctimas del Conflicto Armado, as well as Yolima Quintero and Javier Barrera of ASFADDES Medellín, Héctor Mondragón, Anamaría Lozano, Enrique Daza, Senador Jorge Robledo, Manuel Rozental, Débora Barros Fince, Grace Morillo, Juan Diego Castrillón, the Peace Community of San José de Apartadó, the entire CAVIDA community. Blessed be the memory of poet Piedad Morales. My Colombian friends in Chicago belong here too: Gloria Vélez Rendón, Constanza Valencia, Lina Sánchez and Wilson Herrera, Adriana Posada, Astrid Suárez, Laura and Nathalia Uribe, Bibian Guevara, Elizabeth Lozano, Carol Escobar, and a Colombia Vive Chicago member who has moved south, Adriana Ramirez. Thank you all for your brave work, for pardoning my many failures as an *acompañante*, and for shaping my understanding of both my countries.

I can't forget the longtime friends who have given space to my poems, my love for Colombia, my life: Cindy Bunch, Cindy Kiple, Sally Sampson Craft and Andrew Craft, Deb Keiser, Rebecca Larson, Mark Eddy Smith, Gordon Aeschliman. Steve Bynum and Jerome McDonnell of *Worldview* at Chicago Public Radio have been amazingly supportive. Then there are my recent Colombia travel companions, photographer extraordinaire Michael Bracey and *mujer bella* María Vázquez—you are The Best.

I'm forever grateful to Dan Roche, who invited me to do my very first poetry reading years ago at a Church of the Resurrection coffee house. These days the marvelously multicultural Living Water Community Church is a home for my hybrid soul's poetry and prayer—special thanks to Andi and Al Tauber for always being up for the annual music and poetry garden party.

Muchísimas gracias to my poetry tribe in Chicago, particularly Laura Jean Bailey, Laura Koenig, Lynn Fitz, and Joanne Diaz from Big Table days; so many RHINO poets; and Helen Degen Cohen, Susanna Lang, Renny Golden, and Michael Anderson of City Poets. You have read generously, you have given me clearer vision. I have a beloved tribe in Massachusetts too, especially Molly and Dan Lynn Watt, Martha Collins, Martín Espada, and Fred Marchant, and others, including Lee Sharkey, Demetria Martinez, and Brian Turner, who have opened my horizons at the annual writers' workshop of the William Joiner Institute for the Study of War and Social Consequences.

La gente buena of Glass Lyre Press have treated my poems with great care. Thank you, Ami Kaye and Steve Asmussen, for welcoming and tending this book so well.

* * *

Earlier versions of these poems have appeared in the following publications, to whose editors grateful acknowledgment is made.

Alligator Juniper: "Syllogism"

Avocet, A Journal of Nature Poetry: "Beholding"

CALYX: A Journal of Art and Literature by Women: "Maternal gestures"

Conte: A Journal of Narrative Writing: "Ashore"

The Externalist: A Journal of Perspectives: "Family stories," "Numbers"

Goodreads Newsletter: "After you"

New Madrid: "Flood," "Ride"

Off the Coast: "Soap is political"

Out of Line: Fiction, Poetry, Essays Searching for Peace and Justice: "Our voices, our hands," "Sabbath"

Pilgrimage: Story, Spirit, Witness, Place: "Shrine"

ProtestPoems.org: "Under"

Raving Dove: "Excavation," "For example"

Reunion: The Dallas Review: "Ayer/Yesterday," "Perancho," "Testigo/Witness"

RHINO Poetry: "Arithmetic"

Sin Fronteras / Writers Without Borders: "Eucalyptus"

The Writer's Voice: "Geography of a saint"

Zona de carga / Loading Zone: "Canción de cuna / Lullaby," "Extranjera," "Las horas del corazón"

Glass Lyre Press

exceptional works to replenish the spirit

Glass Lyre Press is an independent literary publisher interested in technically accomplished, stylistically distinct, and original work. Glass Lyre seeks diverse writers that possess a dynamic aesthetic, and an ability to emotionally and intellectually engage a wide audience of readers.

Glass Lyre's vision is to connect the world through language and art. We hope to expand the scope of poetry and short fiction for the general reader through exceptionally well-written books, which evoke emotion, provide insight, and resonate with the human spirit.

Poetry Collections
Poetry Chapbooks
Select Short & Flash Fiction
Anthologies

www.GlassLyrePress.com

www.ingramcontent.com/pod-product-compliance
Lightning Source LLC
Chambersburg PA
CBHW021155080526
44588CB00008B/351